GIFTED

DISCOVERING & DEVELOPING THE DIVINE
POWER WITHIN YOU

JOSHUA R. TODD

The Hope Network Publishing
Garnet Valley, Pennsylvania
www.thehopenetwork.org

ISBN: 978-1-947153-03-5

Cover Design: Allen Oliver | o2Designworks.com

Layout: Penoaks Publishing, http://penoaks.com

Visit the author's website: www.joshuartodd.com

ACKNOWLEDGEMENTS

Thank you to my mother Sharon Todd. Your warrior spirit, love, and passion through life's challenges has helped mold me into who I am today.

Thank you to my beautiful wife Victoria Todd. You are the definition of a Proverbs 31 women. You have taken this hard man and softened his soul to love like Jesus.

Thank you to Bill Levergood for your timely grace and heartfelt guidance through seminary. Your friendship means more to me than my words could ever convey.

Finally, thank you to my Lord and Savior Jesus Christ for taking a wretched, depraved young man and giving him a new beginning. To your name be glory forever and ever!

FOREWORD

The National Retail Federation estimates the average American spends $700 dollars on holiday gifts each year, totaling more than $465 billion. Gift-giving is at the heart of humankind. We give gifts to express outwardly what we feel inwardly to illustrate our love, thoughts, and hopes to the recipient. We communicate to them that they are thought of and loved beyond measure.

The greatest of all gifts is given by God Himself. John 3:16 states, "For God so loved the world, that he gave his only Son, that whosoever believes in him should not perish but have eternal life." A gift is measured by what is given, how it is given and why it is given. What God has given is his most prized possession-his only Son. How he gave him is still being talked about around the world today. Why he has given him is to communicate how much he loves us—he literally thinks we are to die for. But also because he has a mission for us.

God's gift giving does not stop at salvation. God has a purpose and plan for your life. Thankfully he does not call the equipped but equips the called. Upon salvation he provides spiritual gifts not for our enjoyment, but our employment into serving his mission and bringing him the utmost glory he deserves.

In this book, Joshua addresses the many myths, manipulations, and misuses of spiritual gifts. He provides a clear and concise overview of the origination and expansion of paganism while detailing how cults penetrate and pollute Christ's church. He provides a simplistic method to help readers discover and develop their spiritual gifts.

Whether you're a young or mature believer studying in a small group or seminary, *Gifted* will help you fully discover, develop, understand, and implement the spiritual gifts God has given you. If you want to express gratitude for God's gifts in your life, then this book is an important addition to your library.

In Christ,
Dr. Johnny Hunt
Senior Pastor, First Baptist Church Woodstock

TABLE OF CONTENTS

INTRODUCTION: YOUR STORY FOR HIS GLORY

At this very moment as you read the words from this page an almighty, omnipresent, omniscient, omnipotent God sits at every corner of an ever expanding universe watching his creation consummate their story for his glory. With every breath that passes through your lungs so too do the opportunities to glorify God in each moment of your life. Daily obstacles will abound, seasonal storms will rage, momentary mountains will arise to steal your focus from your purpose placing it on your problems. But then in a moment where all time, temptation, struggle, and strife stand still God whispers in your ear, "My child this is all part of my sovereign plan for your story to bring me glory." Different seasons will bring different scenery, but your focus on God should never change. May we all heed the wisdom of an old hymn by Helen H. Lemmel that hearkens us to, "Turn our eyes upon Jesus, look full in His wonderful face, and the things of earth will grow strangely dim, in the light of His glory and grace." There has never been anyone like you nor will there ever be again. Your DNA, fingerprints, talents and spiritual gifts make you one of a kind. Your focus and faith combined with God's favor will pen your chapter in God's story. Claim the salvation freely given to you, embrace the spiritual gifts awaiting you and make your story for His glory worth reading.

OUR STORY FOR HIS GLORY

In October of 2011, God moved my wife and me and our three children just south of Philadelphia to plant a church. The area God called us to was the most poverty-stricken area in America since 1980. It boasted the nation's largest opioid epidemic and overdose rate. The suicide rate was second only to Alaska. Three of the nation's top five most violent cities were within 10 miles. God was literally calling my wife and me to what we often refer to as "the heart of darkness."

Shortly after arriving on the south end of Philadelphia, we started a Bible study in our home. A young man at this Bible study opened up and shared his story. He talked about a life filled with drugs. Ever since he could walk and talk, drugs engulfed his life. He spoke of his parents doing drugs off the kitchen table during dinner and off the coffee table while he would watch cartoons. As he grew older, he and his friends would drink beer and do drugs at the bus stop while waiting for the bus to take them to school. While a high school student, he talked about selling drugs to classmates and trading drugs for good grades to his teachers. Drugs engulfed his entire childhood translating into a career. He didn't know life without drugs. Even as he sat on my couch, he had drugs in his pockets and a gun in his waistband.

A few months later, we met a woman who had been a prostitute since her teenage years. She referred to it as the "hustle of the corner." She spoke of prostitution and the "hustle" that was involved: the mandate from pimps to earn so much a night. She detailed how pimps would intentionally get girls hooked on drugs and would control the accessibility of the drugs in order to get the women to do what they wanted. These women had become enslaved to a substance and to a lifestyle.

That same week a gentleman walked into our place of worship to inquire about our church. As we sat and talked with him, he expressed his desire for life change. He had already embraced a personal relationship with Jesus some years ago but never lived a life worthy of Jesus' calling. We excitedly invited him to become a member of Radiant Church (our church). While out on visitation the following week, he looked over at me and said, "Preacher, if someone shoots me in the face while we're driving around, I want you to know it's not cause I'm getting into trouble." As you can imagine I was pretty shocked and asked him to elaborate. He spoke of a former life of doing very bad things that involved some really depraved situations.

Four months into the launching of Radiant Church, we had a young lady attend a Wednesday night worship experience. It was raining, she didn't look happy to be there. As she sat down, I introduced myself. She responded by telling me she was the mother of a little girl we had baptized a couple months earlier. She urged me to "get on" with church as she was there fulfilling a promise she had made to her daughter. At the end of the service, this young woman raised her hand displaying a willingness to embrace a personal relationship with Jesus. As I walked by her to get my wife to speak with her, she reached out and grabbed my arm. When I looked down at her arm, I noticed track marks up and down her entire arm. I transitioned my gaze to her eyes as she began to weep crying out and saying "I want Jesus! I want Jesus!" It was right there and then she got Jesus! Just as the young man did in my living room and the prostitute did at the altar of our church building.

The young man entered my living room a drug-dealing gang member and left a hope-dealing member of God's family. The prostitute who once viewed her life as an emptying place for men's waste became fully washed clean by the blood of the Lamb. The gentleman who once served depraved men was now serving the Ruler of the Universe. And the young woman who was enslaved to drugs was a living example of freedom in Christ.

I tell you these stories to show you that you matter to God. God cares deeply for you and desires to bring greater purpose to your life. When God saves you, he doesn't just save you from something. He saves you for something and endows you with spiritual gifts to face anything. This book will address the many myths, manipulations, and misuses of spiritual gifts. It will also provide a biblical foundation to understanding and implementing spiritual gifts correctly. But at the end of the book, you will have a choice to make: live as the world leads or follow the Word of God; continue to be a victim or embrace victorious living in Christ and His power. The choice is yours.

PREFACE

When setting a time to meet with the Lord and study this book, I want to encourage you to do these four things:

Meditate: Before you even begin reading, take some time in meditation. Meditation is the process of emptying your mind to focus on an upcoming subject. Meditation will quiet your mind so you can hear God loudly and clearly. Make sure you prepare an environment that will enable you to be free of all distractions. Ephesians states, "For we do not wrestle against flesh and blood, but against principalities, against powers, against the rulers of the darkness of this age, against spiritual *hosts* of wickedness in the heavenly *places*."[1] Our enemy doesn't always attack from the terrifying corners of darkness but through the busyness of life. When it comes time to meet with God, adversaries will clutter your mind with thoughts and agendas, your stomach will growl, or the phone will ring. Something always seems to happen when you have an

---

1   Eph. 6:12

appointment with God. Make sure your mind, heart, and environment are prepared for this meeting.

Examine: Don't just read the Word of God; examine the Word of God. I have heard it said that the Word of God is like a treasure map. More people would read it if they knew this to be true. This proves they have no idea what unspeakable riches it holds. If you were handed a treasure map today, you would undoubtedly hold it very preciously, examining every word and detail leading you to what is at the end of the journey. Understand, God has created you for a journey and the Word of God is His map to help you along the way. Hold it close to your heart, examine it day and night, for it is more valuable than gold itself.

Express: When you have completed reading, take time to express to God what is in your heart and on your mind. Prayer isn't something we have to do, but something we get to do. To think that we get to come before the throne of God Almighty and express what is in our heart and on our mind is truly amazing. As the Word of God is the treasure map to unspeakable riches, prayer is the key that unlocks the treasure chest. Don't pass by any of the riches the Lord has for you. Take the time to unlock and embrace all of what the Lord has for you.

Transform: Information without transformation benefits one little. As the Lord speaks to you throughout each chapter, take time to digest the spiritual nourishment the Lord has given you that transformation may be prevalent your life. Transformation is not a destination but rather part of the journey. Learn to appreciate God's leading in your life in becoming who he wants you to be.

1: THE BACKGROUND AND EXAMINATION OF COUNTERFEIT SPIRITUAL GIFTS

"Now concerning spiritual gifts, brethren, I do not want you to be unaware. You know that when you were pagans, you were led astray to the mute idols, however you were led. Therefore I make known to you that no one speaking by the Spirit of God says, "Jesus is accursed"; and no one can say, "Jesus is Lord," except by the Holy Spirit."[2]

I CORINTHIANS 12:1

Although Paul had already answered many questions and provided divine counsel, the Corinthian Church was still very much divided. The first section of Paul's answers is about carnalities, because their questions were about the things that carnal Christians would be interested in. The carnalities had to do with their factions, wrangling of

1 Cor. 12:1- 3 (All scripture quoted from the NASB unless noted)

different leaders, adultery, lawsuits involving fellow Christians, sexual desires, current fashions, gluttony, and drunkenness at the Lord's Supper. These sins were prevalent in the Corinthian Church and, unfortunately, are often found in the church today.

Paul transitions from addressing carnalities to addressing spiritualties. Rather than focusing on corrective measures for the church, he begins to answer constructively on spiritualties. Paul begins to answer questions about spiritual gifts by emphasizing the oneness of the church. Paul contrasts their experience as worldly idolaters with their present experience as converted Christians. They had worshipped dead idols, but now they belonged to the living God. Their idols never spoke to them, but God now spoke to them and through them by his Spirit.

Very few things are more vitally important to believers than the ministry of their spiritual gifts. These are their God-given endowments for Christian service. Contrary to what many people believe, God's church is not a human organization run for the betterment of society. Nor is God's church a religious club in which people congregate for food, fun, and fellowship. John MacArthur states it well when defining the church:

> The church, as established by Jesus Christ and described and defined in the New Testament, is a living organism. It is the spiritual body of Christ, who is its Head, its Lord. The members of that body are entirely and exclusively those who have become new creatures through faith in

Him as their Savior and Lord. Though composed of human members, it is not a human organization. It is a supernatural organism, created, established, empowered, and led by the Lord Himself. Because its Head is eternal and indestructible, the church is eternal and indestructible. Jesus assures us that even "the gates of Hades shall not overpower it.[3]

The Corinthian Church, like much of the church today, was seriously affected by counterfeiting, misunderstanding, and the misuse of spiritual gifts. Some of the Corinthian believers recognized the problem. Through divine inspiration, Paul continues to answer their questions in 1 Corinthians 12-14 concerning that which they wrote him about.[4] Judging by the apostle's teaching in this section, the questions concerning spiritual gifts include those such as the following: What are spiritual gifts? How many are there? Does every believer have them? How can a person know which gift or gifts they have? How important are spiritual gifts to individual Christian living and to the life of the church? What is the baptism of the Holy Spirit and how does it relate to spiritual gifts? Are all of the gifts given for every age of the church, or were some given only for a special purpose and a limited time? Can the gifts be counterfeited and, if so, how can believers tell the true gifts from the false ones? Paul carefully provides answers to these and many other questions.

3   John MacArthur, *The MacArthur New Testament Commentary, 1 Corinthians* (Chicago: Moody, 1984) 6055.
4   1Cor. 7:1

PAGAN BACKGROUNDS

Just as the Corinthians had perverted almost everything else, they also had perverted the nature, purpose, and use of spiritual gifts. This perversion stemmed from the ideas and practices they adopted from their pagan society and dragged into God's church. Their former lives as unconverted believers were now contaminating their new lives as converted believers. They had not separated themselves from their former ways and were still holding on to that which was "unclean."[5] Although they had become rich in spiritual gifts,[6] they were poor in understanding them and irresponsible in using them. Sadly, little has changed since Paul's writing to the church at Corinth. Believers today are also rich in spiritual gifts but poor in their understanding. Likewise, their irresponsibility in using them stems from pagan societies and cultures.

Today there are thousands of pagan cults worldwide. In Paul's time, pagan cults had geographical roots in Greece and Rome and were part of what are commonly called the mystery religions. These pagan cults had dominated the near eastern world for thousands of years and indirectly would pollute much of western culture.

The mystery religions and all pagan cults have many forms and variations but the same author.[7] In its organized form, false religion began with the Tower of Babel. Cain was the first counterfeit worshiper, many individuals after him followed his example. However,

---

5   2 Cor. 6:14-17
6   1 Cor. 1:7
7   Rev. 17:13

organized pagan religion began with the descendants of Ham, one of Noah's three sons, who decided to erect a great monument that would "reach into heaven" and make themselves famous.[8] The desire to formulate themselves into a singular worldwide system of power and prestige for their own glory was a stepping stone, which all other pagan religions have followed.

From various ancient sources, it seems that Nimrod's wife, Semiramis, was the high priestess of the Babel religion and the founder of all mystery religions. After the destruction of the Tower of Babel and the development of a plethora of languages, she was worshiped as a goddess under many different names. She became Ishtar of Syria, Astarte of Phoenicia, Isis of Egypt, Aphrodite of Greece, and Venus of Rome. Her son, Tammuz, also came to be worshipped under many different names but was most notably recognized as the consort of Ishtar and god of the underworld. According to the cult of Ishtar, Tammuz was conceived by a sunbeam, a counterfeit version of Jesus' virgin birth. Tammuz corresponded to Ball in Phoenicia, Osiris in Egypt, Eros in Greece, and Cupid in Rome.

Several pagan practices were especially influential in the church at Corinth. Perhaps the most prevalent was that of ecstasy. Because it appeared to be supernatural, dramatic, and bizarre, the practice strongly appealed to the natural man. Because the Holy Spirit had performed many miraculous works in the apostolic age, many Corinthian Christians became confused when comparing true miraculous wonders with that of the false counterfeited wonders in the ecstasies of paganism.

---

8   Gen. 10:9-10; 11:4

Ecstasy was held to be a supernatural, sensuous communion with a deity. Through berserk hypnotic chants and ceremonies worshipers experienced semiconscious euphoric excitability in oneness with the god or goddess. Often the ceremonies would be preceded with vigils and fasting and would often include drunkenness.[9] Meditation of sacred objects, vertiginous dancing, fragrant incense, chants, and other physical and psychological stimuli were used to induce the ecstasy, which would be in the form of an out-of-body trance or unrestrained sexual orgy. The trance is reflected in some forms of Hindu yoga, in which the person becomes insensitive to pain, and in the Buddhist goal of escaping to Nirvana, the divine nothingness. Sexual ecstasies were prevalent in many ancient religions and were so much associated with Corinth that the term *Corinthianize* meant to indulge in extreme sexual immorality. A temple to Bacchus (the god of wine) still stands in Lebanon as a witness to the debauchery of the mystery religions.

First Corinthians was one of the earliest written epistles of the New Testament. Although it had been a short period of time since the birth of the church, Satan had begun to confuse believers about any doctrines, practices, and signs. It is imperative to recognize the similarities pagan cults draw with biblical truths as they attempt to create their own deity stories and practices. No matter how much pagan cults try to mimic, manipulate, or distort God's message or methods, his story and his standards stand above all the rest. However, the gullible, worldly, self-centered, thrill-seeking Corinthians with

---

9   Eph. 5:18

their pagan backgrounds were prime targets for the onslaught of Satan to pollute God's pure gospel with a counterfeit religion. It is equally imperative to recognize that Satan does not counterfeit what is not valuable. His attempt to counterfeit the Spirit's gifts are so strong, because he knows they are valuable in God's plan. If Satan can get God's people to become confused and disillusioned about or abusive of those gifts, he can undermine and corrupt the worship and work of the church.

Discernment was one of the chief evidences of the spiritual immaturity of Corinthian Christians. If a cultic practice seemed to have a supernatural effect, they automatically assumed it was from God. If a fortune teller or priest performed something perceived as miraculous, they assumed it was by God's power. Like many Christians today, they believed if something "works" then it must be from God, and it must be beneficial. Thankfully, some of the believers recognized the pollution, division, and immoral practices that characterized many of the members, methods, and messages embodying the Corinthian Church. They asked Paul for wisdom and knowledge in determining what was of the Holy Spirit and what was of another spirit.[10]

---

10   1 John 4:1

2: THE IMPORTANCE OF A CORRECT UNDERSTANDING OF SPIRITUAL GIFTS

Perhaps no area of biblical doctrine has been more misunderstood and manipulated than that of spiritual gifts. Just as the Corinthians had been abusing the Lord's Supper, they also had been abusing their spiritual gifts. Yet no area of doctrine is more vitally important to the spiritual health and effectiveness of the church. It is imperative for Christians to possess a correct understanding of spiritual gifts in order to effectively use them in their intended purposes.

As indicated in the text of most Bibles, the word *gifts* is in italics, which means that that word is not in the original. The term was added by the translators for the sake of clarity; however, the translation can cause more confusion than instruction because of the breadth of the English language.

In order to have a correct understanding of spiritual gifts, it is prudent to understand what the Bible calls them in each context. There are four Greek words. commonly used in the New Testament that refer to spiritual gifts. A look at each one individually will reveal the full meaning of this concept.

1. Charisma

The most familiar term used by Paul is the Greek word *charisma*. Its plural form, charismata, is the word from which we derive in the English language *charismatic*. *Charisma* refers to a gracious work of God or something God has freely given in grace. For example, eternal life is a *charisma*[11] freely given by God in His grace. Likewise, celibacy is also a *charisma* freely given by God in His grace.

2. Pneumatikon

Pneumatikon translated in the Greek means *spiritual things*. This is the word used in 1 Corinthians 12:1 when the Corinthians wrote a letter to Paul asking about spiritual things, Paul responded that he did not want them to be uninformed. Paul wanted to make sure that the Corinthians had a clear and complete understanding of their spiritual gifts, the divine equipment for ministry that the Holy Spirit gives in some measure to all believers for the greater glory of God. Because the masculine and neuter forms of the word are the same, it can indicate either spiritual persons or spiritual things. *Pneumatikon* generalizes all areas of God's gifts not speaking to any particular area of the gifting.

---

11   Rom. 6:23

3. Diakonia

As *charisma* points to the origin of spiritual gifts and *pneumatikon* generalizes them into one category, *diakonia* often translates into *ministries*, pointing to their purpose. All spiritual gifts are designed to serve, help others, and bring glory to God. Particularly, *diakonia* points to the ministry for which the gift was given. For example, in 1 Peter 4:10-11, the verb form is used more than once of gifted believers serving one another. It is important to note that spiritual gifts are not give for personal privilege or benefit but to serve Jesus and serve others.

4. Energema

Spiritual gifts are also described by the term *energema*, translated in the Greek *effects* or *working*.[12] It points to Paul's emphasis on gifts as the effect in ministry or the fruit produced as a result of the working of the gift. All spiritual gifts are energized by the power of the Holy Spirit in and through the believer. Christians are the vessels in which God channels his divine power.

When we combine all four Greek words together, we discover that all spiritual gifts (pneumatikon) are acts of service or ministry (diakonia), which are channeled (energema) in us and through us freely and graciously (charisma) for the greater glory of God.

---

12   1 Cor. 12:6

MYTHS AND MISCONCEPTIONS

When speaking on the topic of spiritual gifts, Sam Storms once said, "Wonderful things in the Bible we see, things that are put there by you and by me."[13] He obviously made this statement sarcastically, but, unfortunately, those words are never truer than when people talk about spiritual gifts. There are many myths and misconceptions about spiritual gifts. We will take some time and examine the most common myths and misconceptions plaguing the church today.

Myth #1-Only ordained pastors or saints have spiritual gifts

False! Paul states in 1 Corinthians 12:7a that to *each one*, male and female, young and old, ordained ministers have all been given the manifestation of the Spirit. Gifts are not exclusive privileges reserved for elders, deacons, pastors, Sunday School teachers, or some specified class of super Christians.[14] The Bible clearly illustrates that spiritual gifts have been given to all genuine followers of Christ despite their title or stature. Aside from the apostles, other Christians who exercised spiritual gifts included 70 followers of Jesus who cast out demons, at least 109 people among the 120 who were gathered in the upper room on the day of Pentecost, Stephen-a deacon, Philip, and Ananias, a layperson.[15] Church members in Antioch who were prophets and teachers commissioned

---

13   Sam Storms, *The Beginner's Guide to Spiritual Gifts* (Minneapolis: Bethany House, 2012, 19.

14   Acts 2:17-18

15   Luke 10:9; Acts 6-9

Paul and Barnabas.[16] Disciples of John the Baptist became followers of Jesus Christ and immediately began to prophesy and speak in tongues. Philip's four young unmarried daughters prophesied. Unnamed brethren of Galatia performed miracles. Believers in Rome, Corinth, and Thessalonica prophesied.[17] As the Bible has clearly illustrated, spiritual gifts are given to every Christian, in every place, in every stature of life.

Myth #2-Spiritual gifts are individual roles

False! Spiritual gifts are not roles. Roles are opportunities for ministry common to all and available to anyone. All Christians are to bear witness but not all have the gift of evangelism. All are to give, but not all have the gift of giving. All pray, but not all have the gift of intercession. All can teach, but not all have the gift of teaching. The same is true with all the spiritual gifts provided by the Holy Spirit.

Likewise, spiritual gifts are not offices. The term *office* is not strictly a biblical one. However, it would appear that an office in the church is characterized by (1) an appointment by the church body, (2) an expectation of longevity, (3) an authorization and recognition, generally by prayer and/or a public ceremony, (4) an appropriate title for the position, (5) compensation for the individual.[18] Offices and roles are positions that one is called to fill; thus it is external. Spiritual gifts are an internal empowerment provided by the Holy Spirit to

---

16   Acts 13:1
17   Acts 19:6; Acts 21:6-8; Gal. 3:5; Rom. 12: 6-8; 1 Cor. 12-14; 1Thess. 5:19-20
18   1 Tim. 5:18-19

carry out God's mission to glorify him in all areas of ministry.

Myth #3-Conversion is the only time a Christian will receive the only gifts they will ever get

False! There is nowhere in Scripture that it states that all spiritual gifts are given at the time of conversion; however, on several occasions[19] Christians are told to desire and pursue gifts they do not yet have. In fact, the pursuit of spiritual gifts is not an optional instruction but a biblical command. Paul writes in 1 Corinthians 12:31 to "earnestly desire the greater gifts." The adverb *earnestly* translated is *zeloo* which means "to set one's heart on, to be completely intent upon." So many Christians view their conversion experience as their arrival point, a destination, the finish line. But a person's conversion is the genesis of a great journey that will test their faith, amaze their minds, and fill their hearts. Praise God for not only laying the path before us but also equipping us for this great journey at hand. Christians should understand the path is rough and the journey will be difficult; therefore, we should eagerly pursue all resources and gifts that God has provided for us that we may make the most of our journey.

Myth #4-Spiritual gifts were given primarily to authenticate apostles

False! The primary, but not exclusive purpose of spiritual gifts, is to edify others *for the common good20*

---

19   1 Cor. 12:31; 14:1, 12-13, 39
20   1 Cor. 12:7

of the saints, the effectiveness of the church, and the glorification of God.

Paul illustrates the purpose of spiritual gifts when he explicitly asserted in 1 Corinthians 14:3 that prophecy serves to edify, exhort, and console others in the church. We find a similar emphasis in 1 Corinthians 14:5, where Paul said that tongues, when interpreted, also edify the church. In 1 Corinthians 14:26, Paul encouraged the brethren to bring a hymn, lesson, revelation, a tongue, or an interpretation when gathering together to worship the Lord. Paul states, "Let all things be done for building up."[21]

It is important to understand that as a believer edifies other believers they will in turn experience blessing and maturity of some sort. Jude 20 instructs believers to "build themselves up." All spiritual gifts were given for the edification, building up, encouragement, instruction, counseling, and sanctifying of the body of Christ. As a believer builds up others and themselves the overall effectiveness of Christ's church is strengthened. The stronger Christ's church is the more power they possess to bring glory to God.

Myth #5-Spiritual gifts aren't necessary now that we have the Bible

False! Spiritual gifts are divinely given qualities to perform useful functions for God, particularly in the area of spiritual service. Just as the human body has members with different capabilities, so individual Christians forming the church as the body of Christ have different

---

21   1 Cor. 14:26

capabilities. Spiritual gifts help individuals contribute to the welfare of the church and overall glorification of God.

On the contrary, the Bible is for information and transformation. The Bible has an inward function where spiritual gifts have an outward function. The Bible cuts to the deepest part of a person's soul to transform them into the person God desires them to be.[22] Although spiritual gifts and the Bible complement one another, each has their own function. Both are vitally important in carrying out God's mission in a person's life.

---

22   Rom. 12:2; 2 Tim. 3:6-17; Heb. 4:12

3: THE CONFUSION OF SPIRITUAL GIFTS

"You know that when you were pagans, you were led astray to the dumb idols, however you were led."[23]

I CORINTHIANS 12:2

The word *pagans* translated in Greek *ethne*, which was commonly used to represent all non-Jews. But in this context, it is representative of someone who is specifically a non-Christian. Paul is drawing a contrast between their former lives as unbelievers to their present lives as believers and followers of Christ.

As former pagans, the Corinthian Christians had once been *led astray to the dumb idols*. The phrase *led astray* translated in Greek *apago* was often used of deceived prisoners being led away to execution. This phrase denotes the understanding that these prisoners were always deceived, always misled, under armed guard, and, in some cases, so weak they were even carried off to imprisonment or execution. Before a person is saved, they are a captive of Satan and imprisoned to their own depraved nature. They are spiritually blind and spiritually weak lacking any power to break the chains of depravity. As Leon Morris puts it, "Pagans are seen, not as people freely following the gods their intellects have fully approved, but as under constraint, people who know no better."[24] It is important to recognize that Morris refers to pagans in the present tense. Pagan is another word for non-Christian and is not just a reference to a people group from the Corinthian's time period.

One of the biggest misconceptions shared by unbelievers and immature believers is that a life apart from Christ is free in contrast with the Christian life, which is constrained with restrictions and guidelines. Paul teaches in this passage, the complete opposite is true. Although an unbeliever may have some choice concerning the type of sin, they are still a captive of sin and Satan. When Paul states, "however you were led" he is saying unbelievers have no choice and no power to prevent sin or escape it.

When I come across this passage, I tend to think of an old friend that I witnessed to on one occasion. I still remember sitting by the roadside in the hills of Pennsylvania. We were both leaving for college the next day, and I knew this would be the last chance I may have to share Jesus with him. As I finished talking, he looked up at me with a tear running down his face and said, "Josh, I believe wholeheartedly everything you just said." To my

---

24   Leon Morris, *1 Corinthians* (Downers Grove: Inter-Varsity Press,1985), 162-163

surprise, I went to respond, but before I could even get a word out, he stated he was not ready. I asked what he wasn't ready for, and he replied, "giving up my freedom." He didn't want restrictions, he didn't want guidelines, and he wanted to do what he wanted to do. I have since then shared the truth that unbelievers are slaves to sin,[25] but he is convinced he is entirely in control.

Unbelievers are not only bound but blind. They cannot see their chains and believe the path they are treading is by their choice not realizing it ends in certain death. Paul gives some further insight in Ephesians: "They are darkened in their understanding, alienated from the life of God because the ignorance that is in them, due to their hardness of heart." Unbelievers think they are free, because they are deceived, unknowingly enslaved to various lusts and pleasures.[26]

People too often seclude pagan worship and idolatry to third world countries. They envision primitive tribesman dancing around a stone or wooden image while shouting chaotically, throwing miscellaneous objects into the air, and lighting burnt offerings. However, pagan worship and idolatry are as prevalent in sophisticated societies today as in any other place in the world. Instead of stone or wooden images, people worship technology, sporting teams, and other materialistic items. Regardless of the dumb idol, each is a slave to sin.

One should give particular attention to Paul's verbiage in referencing the dumb idol. Dumb does not mean unintelligent but speechless. The word *dumb* translated is *aphonos* which means mute, silent, or

---

25   Rom. 6:17
26   Eph. 4:18 ESV; Titus 3:3

speechless. J. Vernon McGee explains, "The idols were voiceless."[27] The psalmist affirms this thought when he states, "They have mouths, but do not speak; eyes, but do not see. They have ears, but do not hear; noses, but do not smell. They have hands, but do not feel; feet, but do not walk; and they do not make a sound in their throat." [28] No idol, primitive or sophisticated, can speak life, love, or any other sweet sound to a person. Nor can it touch the hearts of its worshipper. Idols can neither see, hear, nor walk. They are just as Paul states, "dumb." Whether or not there are demonic forces behind it,[29] an idol is totally helpless to benefit the one who worships it.

The misconceptions of pagan worship and idolatry are a building block of confusion that Satan utilizes to lead captives (unbelievers and immature believers) further away from God. Tragically, this great confusion caused many of the Corinthian believers to fall back into their former idolatrous practices. They could no longer identify the work of God's Spirit from that of demonic spirits or God's spiritual gifts from that of Satan's counterfeit gifts. In doing so, they forsook genuine worship of the triune God for that of pagan idols. They forfeited God's blessings in exchange for nothing from dumb idols.

Just as false spirits, teachers, and doctrines were prevalent in the Corinthian church they abound in the local New Testament church today. Christians must understand God is not a god of confusion[30]. Satan is the

27   J. Vernon McGee, *Thru The Bible, 1 Corinthians Through Revelation* (Nashville: Thomas Nelson,1983), 57.

28   Psalm 115:5-7

29   1 Cor. 10:20

30   1 Cor. 14:33a

author of confusion and his tactic is to mix error with truth to make people more gullible; but a half-truth is still a whole lie. Christian faith is not spiritual gullibility but an obedient response to an objective truth. Satan's strategic plan to confuse Christians about spiritual gifts is a maneuver to prevent believers from discovering and developing the divine power within them. When confusion consumes an unbeliever or immature believer they are just as Paul illustrates: blind, bound, under armed guard being led to certain death and destruction. Thankfully Jesus has victoriously come to set us free[31]. He has provided everyone with a way of escape from our adversaries, truth to test the authenticity of his work, and abundant life instead of certain death[32].

---

[31]   John 8:31
[32]   John 14:6

4: TESTING THE AUTHENTICITY OF SPIRITUAL GIFTS

"Therefore I make known to you, that no one speaking by the Spirit of God says, "Jesus is accursed"; and no one can say, "Jesus is Lord," except by the Holy Spirit."[33]

The clear indication, as recognized by most scholars is that those who were saying *Jesus is accursed* were claiming to be *speaking by the Spirit of God*. Some Corinthians had come to judge the authenticity of the gifts based upon experience rather than content. The more invigorating, showy, unique, and bizarre an act was, the more it was accepted and respected. Many Corinthian believers had fallen deeply back into ecstasy and enthusiasm; however, not all such acts were the result of an opportunist nature. D. A. Carson points out, "It has been argued that some Christians had been dragged before a court and forced to deny Jesus and then, once released, had returned to the Christian congregation and attempted to justify their actions by appealing to the Spirit's leading."[34] The Greek translation for accursed is *anathema* which means a condemnation to absolute destruction. To say that Jesus is accursed is to condemn his nature, his character, his work, his holiness, and his glory to destruction. Regardless of the context or situation in which the words were spoken, Paul's writing to the Corinthian Church serves to remove any justification for the acts or words being spoken.

Although the Corinthian believers had come to the cross to be saved, many of them had not yet moved on to bear their own cross for Christian living. They failed to understand the lordship of Jesus Christ. They failed to embrace the Holy Spirit's commands for the soul's obedience and allegiance to Jesus. Many Christians today stand at the same intersection of obedience and rebellion being torn in opposite directions by their flesh and the Holy Spirit. When standing at such an intersection, I feel it profitable to adhere to the thoughts of J. Vernon McGee's when he said the following:

> Remember the great question which Jesus asked, "Who do you say I am?" Jesus is still asking the same question. You may be of any occupation, any color, any status in life-whoever you are, wherever you are, however you are Jesus asks you, "Who do you say I am?" He asked his disciples that question, and Simon Peter spoke for the group. He said "Thou are the Christ, the Son of the living God." He is the Anointed

---

One. He is the King. He is the Lord. No man
is fit to serve Christ's church unless he has
been mastered by Jesus Christ.[35]

The second part of the verse enhances McGee's
thoughts, *no one can say, Jesus is Lord, except by the Holy
Spirit.* Paul is referencing a genuine confession and
repentance of sin. Anyone can easily utter the word *Lord*,
but as Jesus warned "Not everyone who says to Me, Lord,
Lord, will enter the kingdom of heaven."[36] An authentic
Christian affirms who Jesus really is and obeys His
commands.

The title Lord *kuriou* means deity, master, one who
takes possession and rules over. The word *Lord* is used
around 700 times in the New Testament where the word
Savior is used under 10 times. When a believer makes a
genuine confession and repentance of sin, they must
understand their life is no longer their own.[37] They now
belong to Jesus and are committing themselves to his
sovereign rule.

What a person truly believes about Jesus Christ is the
test of authenticity of a believer's spiritual gifts. The Holy
Spirit always leads people to ascribe lordship to Jesus
Christ in complete obedience, allegiance, and faith, no
matter the place, situation, or cost.

Furthermore, in 1 John 4:1-3 the apostle John
provides a litmus test to A.I.D. (analyze, inspect,
determine) believers against all spiritual deception when
he states, "Beloved, do not believe every spirit, but test the

---

35   J. Vernon McGee, *Thru The Bible, 1 Corinthians Through Revelation* (Nashville:
       Thomas Nelson, 1983), 57-58.
36   Matt. 7:21
37   1 Cor. 7:23

spirits to see whether they are from God, because many false prophets have gone out into the world. By this you know the Spirit of God: every spirit that confesses that Jesus Christ has come in the flesh is from God; and every spirit that does not confess Jesus is not from God; this is the *spirit* of the antichrist, of which you have heard that it is coming, and now it is already in the world. You are from God, little children, and have overcome them; because greater is He who is in you than he who is in the world."[38]

Analyze the source. The manner in which John references spirits here contrasts Paul's speaking of the Spirit of God in 1 Corinthians 12:3. John is not referring directly to demon possession alone, but also false prophets who promote error. Christians have the Holy Spirit and speak for God in union with his Word. False prophets claim to speak for God but are actually speaking by demonic influence[39]. John encourages believers to *test the spirits*. The Greek translation for *test* is *dokimazo* which means to analyze, examine, and verify the authenticity of a source for approval. *Spirits* translates in Greek *pneuma* which means inner being that influences a way of thinking. John is encouraging Christians to analyze the source to verify the authenticity of the inner being that influences a way of thinking.

Inspect their foundation. *By this you know* is a great way to identify spiritual deception is by inspecting their foundation. Does the person stand on a biblical foundation or one of their own intellect? Is their message built by the word of God or the world of humanity? God's

---

[38]   1 John 4:1-4
[39]   1 Jn. 4:3-4

word is the foundation on which he communicates his motive, conveys his message, constructs his method, and completes his mission. The Holy Spirit will never stray from scripture and will always build upon a biblical foundation. False prophets on the other hand will claim erroneous ideas influenced by evil spirits built on human intellect.

Determine what the spirit says about Jesus. *Jesus Christ has come in the flesh* seems to be aimed at Docetism, a false doctrine that states the bodily existence of Jesus and human form of Jesus was a mere semblance without any true reality. This statement may also be aimed at Cerinthus, a gnostic teacher of John's day who denied the supernatural birth of Jesus. He claimed that Jesus and the Christ were separate beings insofar as the divine Christ descended upon the human Jesus at his baptism and departed Jesus before his crucifixion. John contends that Jesus did not merely descend upon an already existing human being, but he entered this world supernaturally as a human being. The Greek tense of the verb *has come* and the meaning of the noun *flesh* indicate that not only did Jesus come supernaturally in the flesh, he was still a human being as John wrote this letter.

False teachers such as Cerinthus attempt to cloud what God has made clear. They embrace the falsehood of fantasy instead of the fruitfulness of faith. They hold tight to the frailty of their flesh instead of clinging to the hope of the cross. They attack the authenticity of God's word and work producing a counterfeit dogma deceiving and leading the masses towards death and destruction. But *greater is He who is in you than he who is in the world*[40]. Believer's need to be aware and alert of spiritual deception, but not afraid, for at the time of salvation the indwelling of the Holy Spirit has given them power over all evil spirits and counterfeit practices. He leads believers into sound doctrine, supplies spiritual gifts, and supplies supernatural power for any task at hand. However, spiritual victory always starts with Jesus. When a person puts their confidence in Jesus it leads to courage from the Holy Spirit and not even the perversions of a believer's spiritual adversaries can overcome them.

---

[40]   1 Jn. 4:4

5: THE SOURCE AND PURPOSE OF SPIRITUAL GIFTS

"Now there are varieties of gifts, but the same Spirit. And there are varieties of ministries, and the same Lord. And there are varieties of effects, but the same God who works all things in all persons. But to each one is given the manifestation of the Spirit for the common good."

1 CORINTHIANS 12:4-7

Paul emphasizes the Corinthian Christians choice to indulge in their flesh rather than the Spirit resulted in quarrels, factions, taking one another to court, immoral and idolatrous practices, polluted marriages and relationships, abuse of their Christian liberty, and became egocentric, heedless, and worldly. Their misuse and misunderstanding of spiritual gifts was a major ingredient to their carnal divisiveness and spiritual immaturity.

The Holy Spirit distributes different gifts to different believers to express and strengthen the unity they have in their Lord Jesus Christ. But misuse and misunderstanding of those gifts shatters unity, divides believers, pollutes their testimonies, and derails their spiritual maturity and effectiveness in the Lord's service to bring Him glory. Warren Wiersbe has an intriguing thought concerning this context of Scripture:

> There is a Trinitarian emphasis here: "the same Spirit... the same Lord... the same God." We individually have different gifts, ministries, and ways of working, but "it is God which worketh in you both to will and to do of his good pleasure" (Phil 2:13). The source of the gifts is God; the sphere for administering the gift is from God; and the energy to use the gift is from God. Why, then, glorify men? Why compete with one another?[41]

Paul spent an abundance of time with the Corinthian believers teaching them about spiritual gifts. But they wandered from his teaching and polluted much of what he had taught. He now reiterates and reinforces what they already should have known and practiced.

Paul explains that the Holy Spirit gives a variety of gifts to be utilized in a variety of ministries that have a variety of effects but a common source and a common purpose.

---

41   Warren W. Wiersbe, *Be Wise* (Colorado Springs: David C Cook, 1982), 137.

THE VARIETIES OF SPIRITUAL GIFTS

"Now there are varieties of gifts, but the same Spirit"

1 CORINTHIANS 4[42]

The word *gifts* here is *charisma in Greek,* which means free and gracious gift. Sixteen of its seventeen New Testament uses are connected to God as the giver. Paul uses it in reference to the gift of salvation, the blessings of God, and divine enablement's for ministry.[43]

Spiritual gifts are not talents. Talents are natural skills and abilities given by God to humankind at the time of physical creation. Because talents are given at the time of physical creation, they are shared by believers and unbelievers alike. An unbeliever can be a highly skilled scientist or carpenter. An atheist or agnostic can be a successful engineer, teacher, cook, or athlete. If a believer succeeds in any related field, it has nothing to do with his or her spiritual gifts. Though they may utilize their natural talents differently after salvation, they possessed them before becoming a Christian.

Spiritual gifts, however, are not natural, but supernaturally given by the Holy Spirit to believers in Jesus Christ at the time of their spiritual rebirth, to share His love and strengthen the body of Christ. Spiritual gifts are special capabilities bestowed upon believers to unify and equip them to minister supernaturally to others, especially to each other. If those gifts are forsaken or

---

42   I Cor. 12:4
43   Rom. 5:15-16; 6:23; 11:29; 12:6

manipulated, the body of Christ is debilitated, divided, and diluted in its quest to carry out the work of God. Os Guinness talks about the importance of the role of giftedness in his book *The Call.* Guinness says, "The purpose of giftedness is stewardship and service, not selfishness."[44] Eric Rees echoes this thought in his book *Shape* when he states, "You were not created to conform. You were not created to compare. You were not created to compete. You were not created to compromise. You were created to contribute to God's kingdom and make a significant difference with your life."[45] Spiritual gifts enable the believer to effectively carry out God's mission in their life.

The understanding that spiritual gifts are free and given by God is a direct challenge and threat to an achievement-oriented humanity that boasts in their ability to do, earn, and obtain. Like Corinthian believers, many Christians today find their identity in their own abilities rather than the one who has created, loved, died, saved, and empowered them. Christians should embrace the spiritual gifts God has uniquely distributed in their lives to make the most of this journey called life. This is best achieved by discovering and embracing that spiritual gifts aren't so much about the believer, but the One who believes in us to carry out his story for his glory.

Believers are tasked with the two-fold responsibility of discovering and embracing their own unique spiritual gifts as well as understanding that God has distributed these gifts in order to promote unity through diversity. If God's church were a football team and everyone wanted

---

44   Os Guinness, *The Call* (Nashville: W. Publishing Group, 1998), 45.
45   Eric Rees, *Shape* (Grand Rapids: Zondervan, 2006), 26.

to play quarterback, there would be a bit of uniformity, but the team would lack the dimension needed to score points and win games. The team could not function if everyone wanted to play the same position. That is Paul's point in this passage. God gives his people varieties of gifts just as players on a team have varieties of positions. These gifts should be utilized in helping make the church stronger to achieve the optimal amount of success.

The word *varieties* translated in Greek is *diaireseis,* which means to divide and/or distribute, in allotments. God distributes his gifts in many forms and varieties to each and every believer. All spiritual gifts fall into two general categories: speaking gifts and serving gifts. The New Testament contains several lists of spiritual gifts (1 Corinthians 12:8-10, 28; Rom. 12:6-8 and 1 Pet. 4:11). One should be careful not to over examine their spiritual gifts. The unique blend of spiritual gifts with culture, position, experiences, and their church body make spiritual tests and surveys unprofitable. Every believer should rest in God's sovereign plan to uniquely gift, shape, and structure them to strengthen his church. John MacArthur says, "Every believer becomes as unique spiritually as his fingerprints are physically."[46]

THE VARIETIES OF MINISTRIES OF SPIRITUAL GIFTS

"And there are varieties of ministries, and the same Lord"[47]

---

46 John MacArther, *The MacArther New Testament Commentary, 1 Corinthians* (Chicago: Moody, 1984), 6331.

47 1 Cor. 12:5

1 CORINTHIANS 12:5

God gives his gifts to be used in varieties of ministries. The word *ministries* translated in Greek *diakonia* means to serve, service, servant, and ministry. Jesus said, "For even the Son of Man did not come to be served, but to serve."[48] Jesus' earthly ministry emphasizes that he came to minister to others for God, and his Spirit distributes spiritual gifts to his people so they can do the same. Spiritual gifts are not a medallion of privilege or prestige but tools for ministry. Charles Ryrie helped bring some understanding of the purpose of spiritual gifts when he stated the following:

> When referring to a gift for service to the body of Christ, a spiritual gift may be defined as a God-given ability for service. God-given reminds us that Christ and the Spirit are the Ones who give gifts; *ability* is a synonym for the concept of a spiritual gift; and for *service* captures the emphasis in the principal passages that gifts are to be used in the serving the body of Christ.[49]

The Lord gives gifts to his servants to serve the body of Christ, and He gives them for a limitless variety of ministries.

Do not misunderstand; spiritual gifts are not given for self-absorption! The focus in serving should always be external for the advancement of Christ's church and never internal for one's own benefit. A person with the

---

48   Mark 10:45
49   Charles C. Ryrie, *The Holy Spirit* (Chicago: Moody Publishers, 1965), 124.

gift of encouragement who never speaks a word or lends a hand unless for their own benefit adulterates their gift. A person with the gift of giving who takes for one's own increase while holding back the Lord's resources is a terrible steward. A person with the gift of discernment who keeps his Spirit-given insights to himself is an unfit servant. A gift exercised in private is a polluted gift. God supplies his gifts to us for his glory. In turn, believers are blessed when they use their gifts to serve others in His name, for His glory, but the blessing is the byproduct not the purpose.

The apostle Peter emphasizes this truth in 1 Peter 4:10 by stating "As each one has received a special gift, employ it in serving one another, as good stewards of God's of the manifold grace of God."[50] We are stewards of God's spiritual gifts. They are loaned to us; they belong to him. God has bestowed upon each and every believer a spiritual gift to be utilized in a variety of ministries. When a believer utilizes their spiritual gifts in ministry they are fulfilling a spiritual need that God has personally equipped them for. Every believer should take to heart that God has called, collected, and commissioned them together for something beyond their own solitary capabilities. God has designed people to do ministry together. For together, the body of Christ is an unstoppable force.

---

50   1 Peter 4:10

THE VARIETIES OF EFFECTS OF SPIRITUAL GIFTS

"And there are varieties of effects, but the same God who works all things in all persons"[51]

1 CORINTHIANS 12:6

Effects translated in Greek *energema* means an effect or activity that is worked out or energized. The One that gives the spiritual gifts also gives energy and power, as well as the faith[52] to make them effective. Just as spiritual gifts have been given supernaturally at conversion, they are energized supernaturally throughout a believer's ministry. No amount of talent, education, or experience will enable a believer to exercise their spiritual gifts in their own power. A believer may exercise their skills, intelligence, and natural abilities in their own power, but only the Giver of spiritual gifts can empower them and make them effective. When a believer attempts to minister in their own power, they risk harming those to whom they are trying to minister as well as the work of God. In order for God's gift to be productive, all believers must be free from sin and be willing to be used. Both the bestowing and the empowering are the Lord's divine jurisdiction; however, one should be quick to remember there is one God who works in all. As Vernon McGee puts it, "The Holy Spirit bestows the gifts; the Lord Jesus Christ administers the gifts—they are under his direction; the Father God supplies the power; and he energizes the gifts.

---

51   1 Cor. 12:5
52   Rom. 12:3

All of this is for the one purpose of exalting and glorifying the lordship of Christ."[53] The Lord has a divine methodology for the distribution, administration, and empowerment of spiritual gifts. Believers should heed the call to purity and obedience to carry out God's divine plan.

The natural man, however, is always more concerned with uniformity than with unity. In their spiritual immaturity and carnality, Corinthian believers were notorious for being superficial copiers. They were more interested in appearance than in substance, and they mimicked those who seemed to be the most noticed, successful, and powerful. Their desire to be successful rather than being submissive, and in being noticed and praised rather than being obedient and faithful, polluted a core component of God's spiritual gifts: unity. God's spiritual gifts have been distributed to promote unity through diversity. Just like the gifts themselves, the energizing of spiritual gifts is sovereignly varied.[54] Gifts may be utilized and energized in countless ways and in many *varieties*. Even the person exercising his/her spiritual gifts will not always see the same process or result when exercising them. Believers should not attempt or expect to have the same gifts or results as other believers. God's people and God's gifts are unique like snowflakes; no two are exactly alike.

The emphasis here on varieties seems to imply that the Corinthians thought that the more dramatic and noticed gifts were the only gifts, or at least the only gifts worth having. Paul instructs them that the Holy Spirit

---

53 J. Vernon McGee, *Thru The Bible, 1 Corinthians Through Revelation* (Nashville: Thomas Nelson,1983), 138.
54 Matt. 13:23

gives a variety of spiritually empowered gifts of equal importance to all Christians. A Christian's concern should be to discover, develop, and dedicate themselves to faithfully using the gift God has given them. God makes no mistakes. He is the ultimate craftsman, story writer, and gift-giver. Believers should rest in knowing God does not create or distribute anything without value. You matter to God, and you play a key role in his story.

As John MacArthur puts it:

> No child in the world could substitute for one of our own children. No matter how many children we might have, none could ever be replaceable. Neither are God's children replaceable or the ministries he has given them replaceable. No other believers can take our place in God's work. He has given no one the exact gift he has given us and he has given no one the exact ministry he has given he has given us. If we do not use our gift no one else will; if we do not fulfill our ministry it will not be fulfilled.[55]

ONE SOURCE AND ONE PURPOSE OF SPIRITUAL GIFTS

> "But to each one is given the manifestation of the Spirit for the common good"[56]

1 CORINTHIANS 12:7

---

55 50. John MacArthur, *The MacArthur New Testament Commentary, 1 Corinthians* (Chicago: Moody, 1984), 6381.

56 1 Cor. 12:7

The manifestation of the Spirit is a reiteration of what Paul has emphasized in each of the three previous verses: God is the source of all spiritual gifts. They are all given by the same Spirit; the ministries are assigned by the same Lord; and the effects are energized by the same God.[57]

Manifestation translated in Greek *phanerosis* means to make known, to reveal, to disclose. That is what spiritual gifts do: they reveal the Holy Spirit and make him known throughout the world. The meaning of *manifestation* is the opposite of hidden or private. Spiritual gifts are never given to be hidden or to be used privately. They are given to manifest the Holy Spirit and to disclose His presence by putting Him on display.

They are also given *for the common good* which translated in Greek *sumphero* means to be profitable to; to be advantageous. Spiritual gifts are to edify and grow God's church stronger while bringing people together in his name. Leon Morris puts it, "A schismatic individualism contradicts the purpose of the gifts"[58]. The focus of spiritual gifts should not be internal on the believer, but external on God's church, for the common good of all.

Not only does the exercise of spiritual gifts minister to other believers but it also enables the user to continually discover and develop his/her own gifts. For example, someone with the gift of giving who faithfully gives generously enables other ministries to be birthed and expanded. Someone with the gift of hospitality who faithfully provides a warm and welcoming environment

---

57   1 Cor. 12:4-6
58   Morris 165

for fellowship refreshes other believers enabling them to be ready to utilize their spiritual gifts. A believer with the gift of leadership who faithfully serves by fostering creativity, casting vision, and applying strategies helps other believers to better identify and utilize their gifts.

However, as believers fail to properly utilize their spiritual gifts, they hinder other believers and ministries while forfeiting the blessings and rewards that come with proper utilization. Some years ago, I attended a teen camp in Summit Lake, Maryland. As indicated by the name, the camp boasted a beautiful lake. I had just spent the afternoon living up to every sport challenge our teenage boys had thrown at us. As the sun was setting, they threw out one final challenge: race across the lake on boats. Each boat consisted of four places for rowers. Because it seemed like an easy challenge, we accepted. However, we only had three counselors so we agreed to take one of the teens as our fourth. Thinking it would be to our advantage, we took Johnny, the smallest and lightest teen. Right from the beginning of the race, we noticed a big problem, our teen didn't feel like rowing. Because he sat idly by doing nothing, his oars just dragged in the water negating the majority of the work the three of us were doing. No matter how hard we tried, we could not make up for the insufficiency of the one doing nothing. We eventually reached the other side and waiting on us were a bunch of cheering teenagers who were so proud of their plan and execution. We argued that had we had a fourth who even attempted to do his part we would have won. We even offered to re-race without a fourth but realized the oars would still just drag in the water. Spiritual gifts and the Lord's church work in a similar way. When everyone doesn't do their part, those that are have to work harder and will still most likely fail. Getting rid of the light kid wouldn't have worked. We needed him to do his part and at least keep the oars out of the water. No matter how insignificant you think you are, the church needs you and you need the church. Together with our spiritual gifts, the Lord's house moves faster and further. The teen who rode in our boat had been emotionally manipulated by other teens to sabotage our race. They told him this was the only way he could be of use and help them win at anything. It broke our hearts. At the end of the week, he came up to us and told us he wanted to race again, but this time he would try. Despite the horror of the last race, we agreed to race again and give him a shot. As the race began, we opened an early lead until Johnny became tired. Although he could no longer row, we instructed him to hold his oars out of the water and allow us to bear the burden of getting to our destination. Johnny complied, and we won the race. If believers are to run a good race and finish their course,[59] we need to do it together. All believers and the gifts God has given them matter. As believers learn to effectively harness every heartbeat, every muscle, every organ, every vessel, every nerve, and every cell together in the body of Christ, they will become a unified, unstoppable movement of God.

---

59   2 Tim. 4:7

6: DEFINING AND DISCOVERING SPIRITUAL GIFTS

"For to one is given the word of wisdom through the Spirit, and to another the word of knowledge according to the same Spirit; to another faith by the same Spirit, and to another gifts of healing by the one Spirit, and to another the effecting of miracles, and to another prophecy, and to another the distinguishing of spirits, to another various kinds of tongues, and to another the interpretation of tongues. But one and the same Spirit works all these things, distributing to each one individually just as He wills"[60]

1 CORINTHIANS 12:8-11

In the present passage, Paul mentions some of those gifts that illustrate the varieties he spoke of in verse 4. This list

---

is only representative of the varieties in this context as additional gifts are mentioned elsewhere in the New Testament, including in verse 28 of this chapter. Paul does not explain the functions of the particular gifts in the present passages. His intention is to illustrate the variety in kinds of gifts and to emphasize the common source of the gifts, of which each is given for, "the manifestation of the Spirit for the common good," stated in verse 7.

As I have previously mentioned, because each and every believer is uniquely made and gifted, the gifts cannot be narrowly defined. We can only provide a general definition by utilizing the terms in Scripture.

The New Testament designates eighteen spiritual gifts, though it nowhere says that other gifts do not exist. To have a full understanding of spiritual gifts, it is important to examine the five passages of Scripture that do identify spiritual gifts:

> "Since we have gifts that differ according to the grace given to us, each of us is to exercise them accordingly: if prophecy, according to the proportion of his faith; if service, in his serving; or he who teaches, in his teaching; or he who exhorts, in his exhortation; he who gives, with liberality; he who leads, with diligence; he who shows mercy, with cheerfulness."

> ROMANS 12:6-8

> "For to one is given the word of wisdom through the Spirit, and to another the

word of knowledge according to the same Spirit; to another faith by the same Spirit, and to another gifts of healing by the one Spirit, and to another the effecting of miracles, and to another prophecy, and to another the distinguishing of spirits, to another various kinds of tongues, and to another the interpretation of tongues. But one and the same Spirit works all these things, distributing to each one individually just as he wills."

1 CORINTHIANS 12:8-11

"And God has appointed in the church, first apostles, second prophets, third teachers, then miracles, then gifts of healings, helps, administrators, various kinds of tongues"

1 CORINTHIANS 12:28

"And he gave some as apostles, and some as prophets, and some as evangelists, and some as pastors and teachers."

EPHESIANS 4:11

"Be hospitable to one another without complaint. As each one has received a special gift, employ it in serving one another as good stewards of the manifold grace of God."

1 PETER 4:9-10[61]

THE TYPES OF SPIRITUAL GIFTS: THE REVELATORY GIFTS

The first five gifts helped start and grow the church. The gifts helped provide revelation of previously unrevealed truths and a powerful ability to communicate those truths in inspired messages. As Robert Thomas puts it, "People became channels used by God to convey His mind to the church."[62] Four of those gifts were wisdom, knowledge, apostleship, and prophecy. Wisdom and knowledge focus more on inward revelations, while apostleship and prophecy focus more on the inspired utterances that resulted from those revelations.

Because of its connection with the gift of prophecy, a fifth gift, the distinguishing of spirits, finds its place in this first category also. Its revelatory aspect lies in the ability of one so endowed to distinguish a genuine revelation from God opposed to a counterfeit one.

The Gift of Apostleship

The gift of apostleship is the God-given endowment to serve and strengthen the body of Christ by planting, birthing, launching, and leading new ministries that advance God's purposes and enrich His kingdom. *Apostle* translated in Greek *apostolos* means a special messenger sent with authority.

People with this gift:

---

61   Rom. 12:6-8; 1 Cor. 12:8-11; 1 Cor. 12:28; Eph. 4:11
62   Robert L. Thomas, *Understanding Spiritual Gifts* (Grand Rapids: Kregel, 1978), 28

- Leaders of leaders
- Ministers of ministers
- Influential among all types of people
- Entrepreneurial and are able to take risks and perform difficult tasks
- Welcome and embrace new challenges

The Gift of Prophecy

The gift of prophecy is the God-given endowment to serve and strengthen the body of Christ by channeling messages of hope, encouragement, conviction, comfort, inspiration, and instruction. *Prophecy* translated in Greek *propheteia* means one who receives a divinely inspired message and delivers it to others in the church. Those who have the gift of prophecy differ from the Old Testament prophets who spoke the authoritative Word of God directly. Their words were recorded in Scripture as they proclaimed, "Thus says The Lord," whereas the messages from those with the spiritual gift of prophecy must be tested.[63]

People with this gift:

- Enjoy publically communicating God's Word
- Have a motivation to share biblical teachings
- Possess a strong conviction to confront heresy and communicate truth
- Speak both boldly and humbly concerning truth
- Possess a strong dependence on Scripture

---

[63] 1 Cor. 14:29-33; 1Thess. 5:20-21; 1 John 4:1-3

- Have a willingness to be broken by God to be better conformed to the likeness of Jesus Christ

The Gift of the Distinguishing of Spirits

The gift of the distinguishing of spirits is the God-given endowment to serve and strengthen the body of Christ by being able to distinguish, discern, judge, or assess a person, statement, situation, or environment. *Distinguish* translated in Greek *diakrisis* means one who is able to make judgements, or possess the ability to decide. *Spirits* translated in Greek is *pneuma* and refers to spirit manifestations. The Holy Spirit gives the gift of discernment to enable certain Christians the ability to clearly recognize and distinguish between the influence and working of God, Satan, the world, and the flesh in a given situation.

People with this gift:

- Recognize the spiritual authorship of a message or situation
- Find it easy to identify pros and cons in any given situation
- Identifies what and how things need to be done

The Gift of Wisdom

The gift of the wisdom also known as the gift of the word of wisdom is the God-given endowment to serve and strengthen the body of Christ by speaking to the life of an individual or specific situation with great understanding and a righteous perspective. *Wisdom* translated in Greek is *Sophia*, it refers to the intimate understanding of the Word of God for righteous living. Psalm 111:10 says, "The fear of the Lord is the beginning of wisdom; all those who practice it have a good understanding. James 3:17 states, "the wisdom from above is first pure, then peaceable, gentle, open to reason, full of mercy and good fruits, impartial, and sincere." God's wisdom is high above and far beyond any other wisdom. All believer's possessing the gift of wisdom or not should seek wisdom from the Lord. However, the Holy Spirit gives some the gift of wisdom to not only impart the truth and understanding to believers, but also to invoke a response of holiness and worship lived out in the world and amongst God's people.

People with this gift:

- Possess a deep understanding of the Word of God
- Enjoy speaking biblical truth into life situations
- Take pleasure in counseling others
- Exemplify a life lived above reproach
- Can apply biblical truth with life experience for righteous decision making
- Uphold God's Word as the mandate and authority for all wisdom

The Gift of Knowledge

The gift of knowledge also known as the gift of the word of knowledge is the God-given endowment to serve and strengthen the body of Christ by communicating an understanding of the things of this world and of the Word of God. *Knowledge* translated in Greek *Gnosis* simply means knowledge and understanding. The scriptural emphasis is one who possesses the ability to communicate worldly and biblical truths in an understandable way.

People with this gift:

- Enjoy studying and doing research
- Devote much of their time to reading and memorizing Scripture
- Possess the ability to relate to life situations and how they correlate biblically
- Delight themselves in answering difficult questions
- Enjoy helping others grow in knowledge

THE CONFIRMATORY GIFTS

Gifts used by God to confirm his divinely inspired messages during the first century include faith, healing, miracles, tongues, and the interpretation of tongues. Confirmatory gifts supported the revelatory gifts and were used to confirm his divinely inspired messages during the first century.

Confirmatory gifts supported the revelatory gifts by giving people a visible means by which to know whether a revelation is from God or not. They emphatically signaled to observers that the miracle worker was from God and had a message they needed to hear.

The Gift of Faith

The gift of the faith is the God-given endowment to serve and strengthen the body of Christ by putting complete trust and confidence in God that allows them to live boldly for him at all times, in all places. *Faith* translated in Greek *pistis* means to have confidence, certainty, trust, and assurance in God. The spiritual gift of faith should not be confused with saving faith. Every Christian who has trusted Jesus Christ as their Lord and Savior has saving faith (Eph. 2:9-10), but only some have been given the spiritual gift of faith.

People with this gift:

- See opportunities when others see obstacles
- Enjoy risk
- Expect God to "show up"
- Pray God-sized prayers
- Are challenged by the impossible

The Gift of Healing

The gift of the healing is the God-given endowment to serve and strengthen the body of Christ by healing and restoring others back to health. *Healing* translated in Greek is *charismata iamaton*, this translation is plural and means gifts of healings. The spiritual gift of healing does not eliminate the need for human science of healing through medical and surgical methodologies. The gift of healing, however, is utilized at various times and places to emphasizes God's love and compassion. The gift of healing cannot be used indiscriminately. If healing is not granted, believers can conclude God has a purpose and plans for allowing the person to go through the illness or infirmity.

People with this gift:

- Possess great compassion for people to be healed and restored
- Possess great faith and trust God can supernaturally heal anyone at anytime
- Utilize human science as a means to help heal and restore anyone at anytime
- Utilize their gift as a platform to point people to Jesus
- Yearn for all people to be in good physical, mental, and spiritual health

The Gift of Miracles

The gift of miracles is the God-given endowment to serve and strengthen the body of Christ through supernatural acts that authenticate God's presence and display His power. *Miracles* translated in Greek energemata dynameon means "working of power, mighty deed." The double plural indicates this gift was diverse and not permanently available at the will of the believer but instead was bestowed at various times and situations.

People with this gift:

- See themselves as a vessel for God's glory
- Utilize prayer as a supernatural vehicle to petition the work of God in the lives of people on earth to reveal his glory
- See opportunity when others see impossibility

- Draw attention to Jesus by the working of his power

The Gift of Tongues

The gift of tongues is the God-given endowment to serve and strengthen the body of Christ by communicating God's message in a foreign language. *Tongues* translated in Greek *glossa* in 1 Corinthians 12:10 means language, dialect, or speech. The gift of tongues and the special capability to speak a foreign language is not previously learned by the one speaking. The style and language type are completed only by divine enablement from God.

First Corinthians 14:22 states implicitly the purpose of the gift of tongues, "Tongues are for a sign, not for believers but for unbelievers." Their ministry is to validate the message and power of the gospel. Because of the visual appeal of the gift of tongues, believers in Corinth unjustly elevated them above other gifts while manipulating their purpose. Just like Corinth, believers today can be found manipulating the gift of tongues for personal attention and glory instead of drawing attention to the gospel and glorifying God.

People with this gift:

- Communicate God's message in a foreign language unlearned by them
- Intercede for others in prayer using unlearned words, sounds, and utterances
- Always speak messages that are profitable to God's kingdom and glory

The Gift of the Interpretation of Tongues

The gift of the interpretation of tongues is the God-given endowment to serve and strengthen the body of Christ by translating a foreign language that has never been learned by natural means. *Interpretation* translated in Greek *hermeneia* means to interpret, explain, or expound a message that is not able to be understood in a natural way. The gift of interpretation is a companion gift of the gift of tongues. By virtue of this gift, a message in a foreign language that was unintelligible could now become intelligible and, therefore, spiritually profitable.

People with this gift:

- Interpret words, sounds, and utterances into an understandable meaning
- Have a clear understanding of what God is communicating
- Apply God's message for his Kingdom purpose

THE SPEAKING GIFTS

The speaking gifts benefit the church in continual growth both numerically and spiritually until Christ's second coming. Although the word *speak* found in 1 Peter 4:9 translated in Greek *laleo* means to say, to talk, to tell, a speaking gift can also be utilized through writing. The speaking gifts contribute to the growth of Christ's body numerically through evangelism while growing the church spiritually through teaching, pastoring, and exhortation.

Each gift is equally important in its function and importance. Evangelism adds members to the body of Christ. Teaching educates members in correct biblical understanding and doctrine. Pastoring provides instruction for righteous living and biblical obedience. Exhortation inspires believers to overcome obstacles and reach their full potential in Christ.

The Gift of Evangelism

The gift of evangelism is the God-given endowment to serve and strengthen the body of Christ by clearly and effectively sharing the love of Christ with others in a way that leads them to repent of their sin and embrace God's gift of eternal life. *Evangelist* translated in Greek *euaggelistes* means one who brings good news. However, it is imperative for all Christians to understand they have been called to share the good news with the lost.[64] Those possessing the gift of evangelism (evangelists) are uniquely gifted in sharing the gospel of Jesus Christ. As Robert L. Thomas points out, "The evangelist will not necessarily have 100% success in his efforts, but he will have a much higher 'batting average' than one who does not have the gift."[65]

People with this gift:

- Look for opportunities to build relational bridges with unbelievers
- Possess a boldness in speaking publically about Jesus

---

64 Matt. 28:18-20
65 Robert L. Thomas, *Understanding Spiritual Gifts* (Grand Rapids: Kregel, 1978), 192.

- Are proud and unashamed of Christ
- Display a lifestyle of grace, mercy, and love
- Are deeply burdened for those who do not know Jesus
- Develop and invest in methods that share the gospel

The Gift of Teaching

The gift of teaching is the God-given endowment to serve and strengthen the body of Christ by educating people in correct biblical understanding and doctrine. *Teaching* translated in Greek *didaskalia* means to teach, instruct, instill doctrine, explain, and expound. All spiritual gifts are equally important as one serves the other, but special emphasis should be attributed to the gift of teaching as it is the essence of Christianity. In the Gospels, references to Christ's teaching ministry outnumber those to His preaching ministry by thirty-three percent. The Gospels refer to Jesus by the title teacher almost fifty times, but never once is He called "preacher." God's Word is at the heart of Christianity with the gift of teaching acting as the lifeblood of the Christian faith. Jesus earthly ministry exemplifies God's chosen method to bring spiritual transformation through biblical teaching.

The spiritual gift of teaching differs from that of natural teaching. Though one may excel in natural teaching, they may not excel in spiritual teaching and vice versa. The spiritual gift of teaching is a special endowment of great importance. Although not everyone possesses the gift of teaching, occasions may arise when every Christian must be prepared to do the work of a teacher.

People with this gift:

- Love studying and teaching the Word of God
- Love seeing others learn and apply God's truth to their lives
- Possess a great conviction to be accurate in biblical truth
- Possess a great ability to present information in a learnable way
- Seek out opportunities to convey biblical truth to daily living

The Gift of Pastoring

The gift of teaching is the God-given endowment to serve and strengthen the body of Christ by taking responsibility for a group of believers and equipping them to live Christ-centered lives. *Pastor* translated in Greek *poimen* means shepherd or overseer. In a biblical context, shepherds have several different responsibilities to their sheep and ultimately to the owner of the sheep. They keep watch for predators and protect the sheep from attackers. They care for wounded and sick sheep restoring them back to health. They seek for them when they are lost and help free them when they are trapped. They guide them to places of nourishment and encourage them to rest. The result of such love and care is a trust-bearing relationship that encourages the sheep to continually follow their shepherd.

Pastors are called shepherds because their calling and gifts align like those of a shepherd. They keep watch for predators seeking to attack and harm their flock. They compassionately care for the hurting, wounded, and sick members of their church. They seek out after them when they disappear and help free them from the grasp of the world, leading them to places of spiritual nourishment. The result should be a flock who trusts their shepherd.

People with this gift:

- Enjoy helping others discover and develop their full potential in Christ
- Enjoy building trust-bearing relationships
- Possess an ability to effectively teach the Word of God
- Yearn to help others in need
- Identify the importance of investing in people

The Gift of Exhortation

The gift of exhortation is the God-given endowment to serve and strengthen the body of Christ by helping others live God-centered lives through inspiration, accountability, admonishment, and empowerment. *Exhortation* translated in Greek *parakaleo* means to beseech, encourage, call upon, and to strengthen. The primary responsibility of exhortation is to remind the listener of the powerful and amazing work of Christ to free them from sin and empower them for his glory. Paul instructs Timothy to use this gift in Titus 1:9.

However, exhortation can take many forms. Exhortation can be to a person or a group of people. Exhortation can be in the form of a warning. In Colossians 1:28-29 Paul states, "Him we preach, warning every man and teaching every man in all wisdom, that we may present every man perfect in Christ Jesus. To this end I also labor, striving according to His working which in me mightily." The word *warning* in this passage has also been translated as *admonishing* or *exhorting.* Exhortation can be in the form of inspiring a person or group to believe in themselves. Exhortation can be empowering someone to take a step of faith.

People with this gift:

- Desire to see people walk a righteous path
- Speak with certainty and finality
- Emphasize Christ's power over the hearer's fear
- Develop opportunities to help others reach their full potential in Christ
- Celebrate others and their accomplishments

THE SUPPORTING GIFTS

Every spiritual gift in its own unique way serves, ministers, and contributes to the body of Christ. The supporting gifts, however, are spiritual gifts that mandate a direct interaction with different members of the body of Christ. They aid and sustain others by supporting them through their spiritual gift.

The gift of helping supports others by physically providing aid to those in need. The gift of mercy supports others by helping one rid distress, misery, and anxiety. The gift of giving supports the overall ministry along with specialized ministries by investing material and monetary substance into spiritual undertakings. The gift of administration supports others by steering others into channels of effective service. The gift of hospitality supports others by providing warm and welcoming environments for others to find peace, rest, fellowship, and restoration. The gift of leadership supports others by casting vision, stimulating spiritual growth, and inspiring progress.

The Gift of Helping

The gift of helping is the God-given endowment to serve and strengthen the body of Christ by providing aid or relief in specialized ways. *Helping* translated in Greek *antilempsis* simply means one with the ability to help. This ability is a specialized service that is applied in a variety of ways. In Acts 6:1-6, the church needed people for serving tables at meal time. The Apostle Paul was personally blessed by Onesiphorus and Onesimus, as they utilized their gift of helping.[66] Others such as widows, orphans, the ill, and poor can benefit from the gift of helping. Although the gift of helping seems like a simplified one, the church of God would not be the same without it.

People with this gift:

- Enjoy serving others
- Explore ways to serve behind the scenes
- Meet needs efficiently and effectively
- Possess a great compassion for those in need
- Celebrate the victories of others

---

66   2 Tim. 1:16-18; Philem. 10-13

The Gift of Mercy

The gift of helping is the God-given endowment to serve and strengthen the body of Christ by ministering to those who are experiencing some kind of distress, misery, pain, or anxiety. *Mercy* translated in Greek *eleao* simply means to show mercy. The gift of mercy contains specialized skills in helping relieve whatever distress, pain, misery, or anxiety another person is going through.

Dorcas of Joppa displayed the benefits gained through a person utilizing the gift of mercy. As Paul sat in confinement, Epaphroditus went and ministered to him in his time of need. Paul emphasizes, "He risked his life to make up for the help you yourselves could not give me."[67] Epaphroditus utilized his gift of helping to minister to the greatest missionary ever when no one else could. This emphasizes the importance and vitality of every spiritual gift.

People with this gift:

- Possess a deep compassion for others in need
- Develop new ways to practically meet the needs of others
- Are sensitive to the feelings and circumstances of others
- Enjoy being there for others
- Possess a unique ability to problem solve
- Are good listeners

The Gift of Giving

The gift of giving is the God-given endowment to serve and strengthen the body of Christ by contributing

---

[67] Acts 9:36; Phil. 2:25; Phil. 2:30

material or monetary substance to spiritual undertakings. *Gift* translated in Greek *metadidomi* means to share, contribute, to give. However, this word is accompanied with the word *generously* which translated in Greek *haplotes* means to give generously, sincerely and without hypocrisy.

This gift provides continual provision for the spiritual undertakings of the church so maximum spiritual dividends may be obtained. Ministry takes two things: people and resources. If people do not faithfully and generously exercise the gift of giving then God's work is like a vehicle without fuel. The vehicle has been designed to move forward, but it lacks the catalyst of resources to get it moving and sustain it.

In Acts 4:34-37, we see the gift of giving exercised wonderfully by believers and a man named Barnabas in particular. Many needs arose in the infancy of the church in Jerusalem. Barnabas sold his land and brought the proceeds to the apostle's feet to distribute to anyone who had a need. The result was the growth of the community and expansion of the church.[68]

People with this gift:

- Regularly give above a 10 percent tithe
- Are excellent stewards of what God gives them
- View their resources as tools to bring God glory and accomplish His work
- Develop new ways to increase their resources to contribute more to God's work

---

68   Acts. 5:12-16

- Are blessed to be a blessing to others
- Find joy in giving to specific needs

The Gift of Administration

The gift of administration is the God-given endowment to serve and strengthen the body of Christ by steering others into channels of most effective service. *Administration* translated in Greek *kubernesis* means to steer, to govern. The meaning here can be personified by the image of a guide who directs his/her followers to a particular destination. Someone with the gift of administration is like a captain of a ship who harnesses the potential of other believers by organizing, directing, and implementing plans for success. This is not a dictatorship. The administrator recognizes their gifts and organizes them, but they still go together.

People with this gift:

- Enjoy seeing people come together
- Are strategic planners
- Possess an ability to see the big picture
- Are self-motivated
- Understand the details to accomplishing goals
- Possess an ability to break a large project down into small pieces

The Gift of Leadership

The gift of leadership is the God-given endowment to serve and strengthen the body of Christ by casting vision, stimulating spiritual growth, and inspiring progress. *Leadership* translated in Greek *proistemi* means to lead, direct, inspire, and care for others. The spiritual gift of leadership is found in Romans 12:8 directly between gifts of giving and mercy. It is placed there intentionally to display its association with caring for others.

Someone with the gift of leadership cares for others by taking the "what is" and casting vision for the "what can be." Charles Stanley states, "The person with this gift might be called a spiritual dreamer in action- a person who can see the intended design of God and turn it into reality."[69]

People with this gift:

- Possess an ability to accomplish a variety of tasks at once
- Possess an ability to inspire others to accomplish a common goal
- Take personal responsibility to care for others
- Can efficiently and effectively delegate responsibilities
- Can identify and utilize the gift sets of others

The Gift of Hospitality

The gift of hospitality is the God-given endowment to serve and strengthen the body of Christ by providing warm and welcoming environments for others to find peace, rest, fellowship, and restoration. *Hospitality* translated in Greek *philoxenos* means the love of strangers.

In the time of the writing of Peter's first epistle, inns were both dangerous and unpleasant. 1 Peter 4:9 instructs

---

69   Charles F. Stanley, *Ministering Through Spiritual Gifts* (Nashville: Thomas Nelson, 2010), 84.

Christians to "show hospitality to one another without grumbling." Someone with the gift of hospitality doesn't just provide a space for use but makes it warm and welcoming. *Grumbling* translated in Greek gongysmos means without complaining. A person with the gift of hospitality does not complain but finds pleasure in hosting others.

People with this gift:

- Desire for people to feel loved, appreciated, and valued
- See environments as opportunities to minister to others
- Promote and coordinate fellowship times and locations
- Enjoy preparing spaces that are warm and welcoming
- Deeply care for both friends and strangers

7: DEVELOPMENT OF SPIRITUAL GIFTS

> "But one and the same Spirit works all
> these things, distributing to each one
> individually just as He wills" [70]

> 1 CORINTHIANS 12:11

There are hundreds of books, surveys, and systems that
encourage Christians to find and fulfill the role of
spiritual gifts; however, there is no indication anywhere
in the Bible that gifts should be sought. That would
contradict both the idea of a free gift of grace that cannot
be earned and the intent of the text, which is to instruct
the Corinthians to recognize that all believers have gifts
that are distributed to each one individually.[71]

God's gifts are not a buffet for believers to come and
choose from as they desire but a divine gift energizing the
believer for the works of God. *Works* translated in Greek

---

70   1 Cor. 12:11
71   1 Cor. 12:11

energro means to cause to function, to grant the ability to. The Corinthians were fascinated with tongues and obsessed with seeking out and practicing spiritual gifts God had not given them. This polluted and distorted the purpose and plan of God's working, creating a competition-driven culture instead of a unified one. A believer should not be consumed with what gifts God has given them but focus on developing how to use that which He has given. In doing so, the focus transitions from the tool to the craftsmen. Much joy should be brought to the heart of a believer to know Who lives in them is seen by what they do. Kent Hughes helps bring perspective:

> God himself overcomes our achievement-centered culture by giving himself away. Our identity itself is a gift to be received. This allows sinners to give up their attempts to earn status and position. This also allows sinners to view others as inherently valuable regardless of status or position. One's abilities, skills, and gifts are all the result of grace-they are given. This allows Christians to be humble. We did not earn what we have. This allows Christians to invest because our gifts are for the purpose of the common good. Individuals no longer gift-grab because they have been given all they need.[72]

---

72   Kent R. Hughes and Stephen T. Um, *1 Corinthians* (Wheaton: Crossway, 2015), 217.

Spiritual gifts are not just about what God has given, but why he has given them. God has not saved you to sit and do nothing. God has saved you to serve. Through his sovereign control of spiritual gifts, he has uniquely equipped each and every believer for the tasks at hand.

Although the Spirit is the source of spiritual gifts, believers have a part in the development of their gifts. Charles Ryrie states, "The Holy Spirit is sovereign in the giving of gifts, but in the development of them he works through human beings with their desires, limitations, ambitions, ability to discipline themselves, and the like."[73] Believers must bear the responsibility to discipline themselves to continuingly G.R.O.W. (gain, recognize, own, work) and develop their spiritual gifts.

Gain understanding. Before you can utilize your spiritual gifts you must first gain a firm understanding of what spiritual gifts are. A poll conducted on social media by The Hope Network revealed that less that 10% of Christians even know what spiritual gifts are. Less than 1% could name and number the spiritual gifts. The reality of ignorance concerning spiritual gifts in relation to Christian living is alarming. If Christians are not aware of the God-given endowments bestowed upon them for service, how then can they develop them? The "defining and discovering" section of this book is a great resource for Christians to gain understanding of spiritual gifts.

Recognize your gifts and opportunity for service. Because the Bible does not detail any one method to discovering spiritual gifts, believers should participate in various ministries to which they feel drawn. Rick Warren

---

73   Charles C. Ryrie, *The Holy Spirit* (Chicago: Moody, 1965), 127.

advises, "The more you serve God in ministry, the more clearly you will see your gifts." [74] Ask God for direction, and then ask your church leadership for suggestions and start serving. As you serve and experiment with different ministries, you will recognize what your gifts are and where you should be utilizing them.

Own. Too many Christians occupy space rather than taking ownership of service. If a Christian is sitting and not serving than they are probably not believing. They are not believing in the ministry, the leadership, the direction of the church or even genuine belief in Christ and his Word. The possibility for disbelief is endless but so are the accomplishments for Christ's bride when servants stop occupying space and start taking ownership of service. No one will get to heaven because of a profession of faith, they need possession of faith. If a Christian truly wants to develop their spiritual gifts, they will aim to claim that which God has given them.

Work. The *Washington Post* detailed Americans' lack of time and work put in at any religious activity: "We average just four minutes on religious and spiritual activities on Monday through Friday- about the same amount of time we spend tossing and turning in our sleep. Not surprisingly, religious practices spike on Sunday. But even on Sundays, Americans spend more time grooming themselves than they do praying or going to church."[75] Ministry is hard work that takes time and dedication. Ministries will not thrive on spare time and spare change; they require passion, perseverance, and

---

74   Warren W. Wiersbe, *Be Wise* (Colorado Springs: David C Cook, 1982), 241.

75   Christopher, Ingram. "How you spend your days America- In 10 charts." The *Washington Post (2014):* Washingtonpost.com/wonkblog (June 27, 2014)

performance. If a believer desires to grow their spiritual gifts, they must be willing to put in the work.

8: YOU MATTER

"For even as the body is one and yet has many members, and all the members of the body, though they are many, are one body, so also is Christ"[76]

1 CORINTHIANS 12:12

The body is composed of many members. There are bones and muscles, flesh and blood, nerves and tendons, and glands and organs. I am reminded of how vitally important every member of the body is when I think back to my senior year of high school. I was wrestling in the championship of a tournament my high school was hosting. My opponent was the number three ranked wrestler in the county. My record at the time was 17-1 with my soon-to-be opponent representing my only loss. As I walked out onto the mat, I had never been more focused or confident in my life. The match started with me taking him down and almost turning him right to his back. I let him up, and a few seconds later, I took him down once again. Because of my dominance from the neutral position, my coach told me to let him up and take him down to maximize points. However, after I let him up the third time, he shot in to take me down. I sprawled backwards, something I had literally done thousands of times throughout my wrestling career. But when my foot hit the mat, an old toe injury reoccurred causing my leg to twist in an unorthodox way. As we rolled out of bounds, I went to stand up and couldn't. The pain wasn't that bad, but my leg just didn't want to work. I had to finish the match without standing up which resulted in me losing a close match. I later went to a specialist who explained to me that the lack of support from my toe caused my leg to become injured. Because my toe wasn't functioning at 100%, my leg had been bearing a heavier burden. There were no implications at all, no pain, no swelling, nothing! Then one day at one of the most vital times in my sporting career, a ligament in my leg tore. My doctor explained to me that my wrestling career was done and that I would have to do two years of rehabilitation to fully recover back to full health. I had spent many years lifting weights, running, stretching, and dieting correctly but never realized how important my big toe was to my health. Against my doctor's advice, I finished the season by greatly underachieving. I remember sitting in the stairwell weeping after my final match. My leg was black and blue, and I could barely walk, but the physical pain was nothing compared to the emotional pain.

There are many members in the human body. Not all of them stand out when a power lifter lifts a record weight, a track star sprints to the finish, or even when a wrestler sprawls from an incoming shot. But each and every member of the body matters. Just as there are many members in the physical body, there are many members in the body of Christ. Not every member gets outspoken praise and affirmation; some are the toes and ligaments that go unnoticed. But every member matters, and when one refusers or is unable to do their job, the rest of the body suffers.

Paul is using this passage of Scripture to illustrate the unity and interconnection of the members of Christ's body. Paul uses this illustration many times in his writings.[77] The human body is marvelously complex yet unified. The members operate in complete harmony with one another. The body cannot be subdivided into different bodies. If one part is cut off, then it ceases to function and dies, leaving the rest of the body weakened and unable to function in full effectiveness. As a Christian, your life has purpose. God hasn't just saved you from something, He has saved you for something and has gifted you for anything. You matter to God and you matter to his church. If you refuse or become unable to fulfill your role within the body of Christ, the body will suffer. If any believer is in an unhealthy state in his/her life, they should seek restoration as soon as possible. I often think how my wrestling career would have ended had I given complete attention and care to my toe. It's often the little things we think we can control that cause the most damage. No matter how big or small something

---

77   Rom. 12:5; Eph. 1:23; 2:16; Col. 1:18

may seem, give it the attention it needs and restore it back to full health. Your body needs you!

A FINAL CHARGE

Throughout this book we have exposed and debunked the myths, misuses, and manipulations of spiritual gifts. We have examined the origination and expansion of paganism. You have been educated on the various types of spiritual gifts and their purposes. The question now is what will you do with such knowledge? Will you simply disregard the gifts God has given you or will you discipline yourself to continually discover and develop them all to the greater glory of God? The choice is yours.

BIBLIOGRAPHY

Bible Gateway: 1 Corinthians 12 (NASB). https://www.biblegateway.com

Blomberg, Craig L. *The 1Corinthians NIV Application Commentary.* Grand Rapids: Zondervan,1994.

Carson, D.A. *Showing* the *Spirit, A Theological Exposition of 1Corinthians 12-14.* Grand Rapids: Baker Academic, 1987.

Carson, D.A. *The Cross and Christian Ministry, Leadership Lessons From I Corinthians.* Grand Rapids: Baker Books, 1993.

Evans, Roderick L. *The Spiritual Gifts, A Biblical Explanation of the Gifts of the Spirit.*

Camden: Abundant Truth, 2014.

Guinness Os. *The Call, Finding and Fulfilling the Central Purpose of Your Life.* Nashville: W. Publishing Group, 1998.

Hughes, Kent R., and Stephen T. Um. *1 Corinthians, The Word of the Cross.* Wheaton: Crossway, 2015.

Ingram, Christopher. " Here's how you spend your days, America- in 10 charts." *Washington Post* (2014): Washingtonpost.com/wonkblog (June 27, 2014).

MacArthur, John. *MacArthur New Testament Commentary, 1 Corinthians.* Chicago: Moody, 1984.

MacArthur, John. 1 Corinthians, godly Solutions for Church Problems. Nashville: Thomas Nelson, 2007.

McGee Vernon J. *The Epistles First Corinthians.* Nashville: Thomas Nelson,1991.

McGee Vernon J. *Thru The Bible, 1 Corinthians Through Revelation.* Nashville: Thomas Nelson, 1983.

Morris, Leon. *1 Corinthians.* Downers Grove: Inter Varsity Press, 1985.

Ryrie, Charles C. *The Holy Spirit.* Chicago: Moody Publishers, 1965.

Phillips, John. *Exploring 1 Corinthians, An Expository Commentary.* Grand Rapids: Kregel Publications, 2002.

Rees, Erik. *Shape, Finding and Fulfilling Your Unique Purpose for Life.* Grand Rapids: Zondervan, 2006.

Stanley, Charles F. *Ministering Through Spiritual Gifts, Recognize Your Spiritual Gifts and Use Them to Further the Kingdom.* Nashville: Thomas Nelson, 2010.

Storms, Sam. *The Beginners Guide to Spiritual Gifts.* Minneapolis: Bethany House, 2012.

Study Bible ESV. Wheaton: Crossway, 2008.

Thomas, Robert L. *Understanding Spiritual Gifts, A verse by verse study of 1 Corinthians 12-14.* Grand Rapids: Kegel Publications, 1978.

Wiersbe, Warren W. *Be Wise, Discern the Difference Between Man's Knowledge and God's Wisdom.* Colorado Springs: David C Cook, 1982.

Made in the USA
Columbia, SC
09 February 2018